Original title:
Searching for Purpose in All the Wrong Places

Copyright © 2025 Creative Arts Management OÜ
All rights reserved.

Author: Arabella Whitmore
ISBN HARDBACK: 978-1-80566-008-8
ISBN PAPERBACK: 978-1-80566-303-4

The Hollow Pursuit

In a quest for glittering gold,
I tripped over shoelaces old.
My map was drawn in crayon bright,
But led me straight to a cat's bite.

I chased my dreams like a speedboat,
Over puddles that looked like moat.
With each new turn, I lost my way,
But laughed at life's silly ballet.

Hopes Entangled in Thorns

A garden plant I thought would bloom,
Instead, it turned into a broom.
With every poke from thorny vines,
I mused on love as I drank wines.

I searched for joy among the weeds,
But found only tangled misdeeds.
Each petal whispered tales of woe,
As I dove head-first into the show.

Fragments of Forgotten Dreams

I found old dreams beneath my bed,
To dust them off, I patted dread.
They whispered hints of grand designs,
But mostly just asked for some wines.

In faded pages lost and torn,
Were jokes about the day I was born.
I laughed and cried till both ran dry,
In a circus clown's suit, oh my!

The Treasure Map to Nowhere

A treasure map with x marks clear,
Led me to my neighbor's deer.
I dug up bones from ancient days,
And found my lunch from last Wednesday's craze.

With every clue, my hopes would swell,
Only to find a jingle bell.
I tiptoed home with empty hands,
Still dreaming of my pirate plans.

Chasing Rainbows Without Rain

I chased a rainbow down the street,
Hoping for gold at my little feet.
But all I found was a soggy shoe,
And a cat who thought it was meant for a chew.

In the sky, a color show bright,
But my wallet's been empty all night.
Was there a pot to be won? Who knows!
I'm stuck with a cat and a garden hose!

Climbing Mountains Made of Sand

I thought I'd climb the tallest dune,
With dreams of victory under the moon.
But every step felt like a slide,
And I ended up kicking my pride aside.

I built a castle, oh so grand,
Only for waves to take a stand.
A royal ruin in a tide's embrace,
Turns out, my kingdom's a split-second race!

The Allure of Mirage

I saw a feast just off the path,
A mirage so real, I felt its wrath.
I reached for burgers, fries, and shakes,
But ended up tripping on my own high stakes.

In the desert heat, my eyes played tricks,
Thought I found heaven, just a bag of bricks.
I laughed aloud at a ghostly spread,
Turns out my diet loves to misled!

Paths of Ashes and Shadows

I wandered paths where shadows danced,
With hopes and dreams carelessly pranced.
But ashes swirled, like confetti gone bad,
I picked up my spirits, though slightly miffed and mad.

In the twilight glimmer, I lost my way,
Thought I'd find answers, but found dismay.
So here I am with shoes worn thin,
Still stepping forward, maybe I'll begin!

The Quest of the Lost Souls

In the cupboard of socks, I thought I'd find gold,
But only old lint and a story retold.
I searched in my fridge, for a reason so grand,
But the only thing twinkling was last week's jam.

Among Fragments of Hope

Wandered through aisles with a list made of dreams,
Found a great deal on some canned refried beans.
Tried to catch clouds with a net from my shed,
But they floated away, leaving me with a thread.

When Horizons Fade to Gray

I looked in the mirror for wisdom and cheer,
But the face that looked back just grinned ear to ear.
The ticket was punched for a wild, crazy ride,
But it's just me and my cat, alone for the slide.

The Eternal Drift of Yearning

I asked a magician for a hint of my fate,
He pulled out a rabbit and said, "Just wait."
So I sat on a bench with my hopes all in tow,
And watched pigeons plot for their next grand show.

The Mirage of Meaning

I bought a map that led to bliss,
But all I found was a rubber fish.
My compass spun in circles tight,
It pointed left, but I turned right.

The signs ahead all read 'nowhere',
I took a shortcut, met a bear.
He asked me what I hoped to find,
I shrugged my shoulders, peace of mind.

I baked a cake, hope it was sweet,
But frosting flopped on my two left feet.
I danced with joy 'til I was sore,
And wondered what I wanted more.

So here I am, with knotted strings,
Chasing shadows, laughing at things.
Perhaps the joke is on my face,
In every corner, I've lost my place.

Echoes in Empty Rooms

I wandered through a house of jokes,
Where laughter bounced like rubber blokes.
I shouted loud, 'Are you in there?'
Just echoes answered, 'Go grab a chair!'

I stepped on toys, heard plastic squeak,
Pondered if the walls could speak.
'Does meaning hide behind the fridge?'
I found a note, 'Just take the bridge!'

I played with shadows on the wall,
Pretended that I was so tall.
But mirrors cracked from too much glee,
And once again, it's all on me.

So here I sit, with crumbs and dust,
In quest of wisdom that I must,
The echoes laugh, their voices loom,
In this absurd, abandoned room.

Wandering Through Misty Roads

I drove my car on paths unseen,
With GPS that turned to green.
It said, 'Recalculate!' with grace,
I waved at cows and lost my place.

The rain danced down, the fog rolled in,
I took a left, found my best grin.
A puddle splashed as I found a stone,
'Is this the journey? Am I alone?'

The signposts teased with riddles quaint,
A cow in shades, a goat in paint.
I rolled my eyes, then stopped to muse,
Should cows wear shades or am I confused?

So off I went through misty bends,
Where every curve just shakes and bends.
I might not learn what I seek today,
But giggles paint this cloudy gray.

Yearning for Clarity

I wore my glasses but couldn't see,
The world was fuzzy, like my cup of tea.
I flipped my hair, thought that was the key,
But clarity fled, dancing with glee.

I tried meditation atop a hill,
To find great truths, but fell down still.
The breeze just laughed as it tousled my hat,
It whispered secrets: "You're funny like that!"

A wise old man on a rocking chair,
Said, 'Life's a circus; embrace the dare.'
I juggled dreams, but dropped them all,
And in my laughter, I heard the call.

So here I twist, in a spiral dance,
Chasing insights on a wild chance.
In this chaos, I find the light,
With every giggle, I feel alright.

The Search Beyond the Horizon

I bought a map that led nowhere,
A compass that pointed to despair.
I tripped on dreams left in the dust,
And laughed at plans that turned to rust.

I wandered through a maze of thought,
With every twist, I found I fought.
A sandwich shop became my guide,
Where mustard and mayo coincide.

I chased the sun, but it was shy,
It hid behind a pizza pie.
The universe laughed, a cosmic tease,
As I tripped over my shoelaces with ease.

In this grand quest for that one thing,
I found a frog that liked to sing.
He croaked out wisdom, ribbit by ribbit,
And I forgot my goals—oh, what a limit!

Paths of Endless Nights

I stumbled down a road of socks,
Where mismatched pairs made quite the blocks.
The moon wore shades, so cool and bright,
I asked it if my path was right.

I met a cat who spoke in rhymes,
Claiming he knew all the best times.
He nibbled cheese and danced in place,
While I just tried to keep up the pace.

A pizza slice became my muse,
In sauce and cheese, the path confused.
With every bite, the night grew bold,
And my ambitions turned to cold.

At dawn, I found my way back home,
With tales of nights when I would roam.
Perhaps the quest was just to play,
In oddities, I'd found my way.

A Dance on Broken Glass

With tap shoes on, I hit the floor,
In a shattered hall, I danced and swore.
Each step a crunch, each spin a laugh,
While others stared, I chose my path.

I twirled around, in sparkles bright,
No cuts or bruises, just pure delight.
The pieces sang a jumbled tune,
As I boogied beneath the moon.

A jester joined, with juggling flair,
He tossed the shards like they were air.
We sparkled and laughed, what a fine jest,
In clumsy turns, we danced our best.

So here I am, in a glassy mess,
With moves so wild, they leave you guess.
In every glitch, I find my chance,
To waltz in chaos, join the dance.

Fleeting Glimpses of Certainty

With a telescope aimed at my fate,
I saw a carrot on a plate.
It danced away, just out of sight,
Leaving me giggling in the night.

I hunted clues in cereal bowls,
Where marshmallows hid like secret goals.
Each crunch revealed a minor clue,
But all I found was sticky goo.

A unicorn told me, "Just relax,
Life's not a puzzle, quite the wax!
So ride the waves of what you feel,
And trust in laughter—it's the deal!"

So I frolicked in this silly quest,
Chasing whims like a jester's jest.
In every fleeting glimpse I see,
Perhaps it's joy that sets me free.

Timeless Wanderings

I wandered through a garden fair,
Chasing dreams that danced in air.
A butterfly with sunglasses on,
Said, "You've got it all wrong, friend! Come on!"

I sailed my boat on a cereal sea,
Hoping goldfish would welcome me.
A parrot squawked, "Just aim for the sun!"
I threw my map, guffawed, then ran.

I took a stroll down a cookie street,
Where did my purpose and biscuits meet?
A chipmunk laughed, "You've missed the clue,
It's not in there, it's in the stew!"

In dreams of shoes that danced on air,
I tripped on clouds, without a care.
The moon just grinned, "You're quite the case,
But fun is found in the silliest place!"

A Journey Through the Fog

In shadows thick, we roam around,
With maps that lead to lost and found.
A compass spins, where should I go?
The only guide? A friendly crow.

We trip on rocks and slip on mud,
Chasing dreams that seem like a dud.
The trail's a joke, a jolly prank,
Who knew the path would stank so rank?

We laugh aloud, the fog won't clear,
But hey, at least we've got some beer.
With every turn and every twist,
Life's a party, not to be missed!

So here's to the fog, the laughter bright,
In all this chaos, we just might
Find joy in puddles, and that's the key—
Embrace the nonsense, wild and free!

The Illusion of Golden Horizons

Chasing sunsets, oh what a sight,
But where is gold? Not in this light!
The horizon glows, a tempting tease,
Yet all we find are wilting trees.

With spoons in hand, we dig for dreams,
Only to find they burst at seams.
A fortune cookie told me once,
'Look for gold!'—now who's the dunce?

We wander fields of daisies bright,
Hoping to strike it rich tonight.
But instead of loot, we found a shoe,
Guess it was mine—I knew that too!

So let's toast to our silly chase,
For who needs gold when we have grace?
In every stumble, a laugh we gain,
Life's a strange, delightful game!

Grappling with Ghosts of Yesterday

In the attic sit my past regrets,
Dusty boxes, no cash bets.
I talk to ghosts, they shout and jest,
'You think that's tough? Just try our fest!'

With poltergeists giving life advice,
I'm trapped in tales of roll the dice.
They say to grow, then retell the tale,
But all I hear is their wailing wail.

We dance around in sheets so white,
Scaring kids who run in fright.
Yet there's a comfort in every scream,
In haunting echoes, we find our dream.

So here's to the past, both grim and grand,
With humor lurking, hand in hand.
Embrace the ghosts, let laughter flow,
Chase the shadows, enjoy the show!

The Maze of Misplaced Hopes

In a maze of choices, left and right,
I lost my socks, it doesn't feel right.
With walls of doubt, I twist and turn,
Who built this place? I have much to learn!

A sign points west, the east says stay,
Should I trust my shoe or my gut today?
With every step, I'm led astray,
Lost like that sandwich—where'd it stray?

Yet in this maze, my giggles bloom,
As I dodge life's metaphorical broom.
Around each corner, a brand new mess,
But oh, the joy in this crazy stress!

So here I dance in my tangled fate,
With misplaced hopes, I don't much rate.
But fun's my compass, let laughter guide,
In this maze of life, I'll take it with pride!

Hearts Adrift in the Dark

In the closet of dreams, I found a sock,
Maybe it holds the answers, or just ticks and tock.
A treasure map scribbled on a napkin fierce,
Led me to a taco stand, and oh, how I pierce!

Under my bed, a world unknown hides,
With dust bunnies plotting to take me on rides.
A sandwich I lost turned into a quest,
If only I knew what I searched for, at best.

The Allure of Distant Horizons

The view from the roof, a sight so unclear,
Thought I'd find wisdom but got leftover beer.
Chasing the clouds, a whimsical flight,
Only to tumble into a pillow fight!

Horizons expanded, my dreams took a leap,
Found a rubber chicken, not wisdom to keep.
A map full of 'X's led me astray,
Turns out the prize was just yesterday's clay.

Misguided Routes

I asked a goldfish for a sound piece of advice,
It blinked and swam, the fishy little slice.
Wandered through alleys looking for signs,
Ended up in a shop selling glittery vines.

GPS in my phone, it took me for a spin,
Directed me straight to a place made of tin.
Some say it's fate, others call it a joke,
Found a rubber band ball, thought that was a poke.

Searching for Gold in Gravel

I sifted through gravel, Eager for change,
Found a coin from last year, oh how it's strange!
Thought I'd strike gold, but found only sweat,
And a pebble that glimmered, just as my pet bet.

Tried serious digging with a spoon and a grin,
Hoping for riches where rubbish had been.
Turns out the real treasure, I learned in a flash,
Is laughter and snacks, not a pile of cash.

The Siren Song of False Paths

I followed a map made of cake,
Each sweet crumb led me to heartbreak.
No treasure to find, just frosting and sprinkles,
I danced with my dreams, but all I got was crinkles.

The lighthouse shined bright but it was a mirage,
I found a lost sock instead of a collage.
With each twist and turn, I giggled and blundered,
Who knew life's quest could leave you so thundered?

I knocked on doors that went straight to the wall,
Wished for a party, but got a buffet stall.
I searched for the stars, tripped over my shoe,
And learned that my path had a laugh track too.

So here's to the fools who wander with glee,
Finding all joy, from calamity's spree.
Next time I wander, I'll cherish the ride,
For laughter's the compass, and dreams are the guide.

Where the Compass Sways

At the crossroads, the compass just spins,
I'm lost in the logic of what makes sense wins.
It pointed to pizza, then ice cream so bright,
Took a left at my sanity, and ended the night.

Tangled in vines of my wild imagination,
Thought I'd find wisdom in a vacation.
An octopus chef and a kangaroo friend,
Who knew all my travels would just make me bend?

Found wisdom in fortune cookies galore,
But each crunch brought questions, not the answers I score.
I dived into oceans of absolute daze,
With maps that unfold in a bewildering blaze.

Next time I'll follow the giggles and grins,
Through mazes of nonsense life often spins.
For purpose is humor, and jokes are the key,
In this compass of chaos, I'll let it lead me!

Navigating the Labyrinth of Longing

In a maze of desires, I stumbled anew,
Looking for meaning, but found a weird zoo.
A penguin was dancing, a monkey played lute,
I pondered my life while I stepped on a boot.

Each corner I turned brought a giggle and sigh,
A poodle in glasses was giving me high.
With every odd turn, a lesson I found,
Purpose is humor wrapped up in the sound.

Chasing some dragons that turned into flutes,
I searched for the truth, while riding on coots.
But the laughter that bubbled from deep in my chest,
Was the real North Star leading to my best.

So laugh through the maze, let your heart be the map,
For joy in the journey is the smartest of traps.
In the labyrinth of life, look for the odd,
Where purpose is found in the whimsy of God.

The Delusion of Stardust

Caught in the sparkle of glitter and dreams,
I searched for the cosmos, or so it now seems.
A star that I wished upon turned into cheese,
And the universe giggled as I sneezed with ease.

I tried to catch rainbows and ride on the gusts,
But all that I gathered were crumbs and weird dust.
The planets were laughing; it seemed quite a riddle,
While I chased my tail and played acrobatic fiddle.

Chasing horizons with shoes made of glass,
I thought I'd find wisdom but fell on my sass.
Each tumble was met with a cosmic high five,
As the universe chimed, "Hey, just be alive!"

So here's to the stardust we suppose can guide,
With a wink and a twist, let giggles abide.
For in this delusion of knowing our fate,
The fun in our folly is what makes life great.

Wanderlust Without a Map

I wandered off to find my goals,
With ice cream cones and playful strolls.
Each sign I saw just pointed south,
To donut shops, with a sprightly mouth.

A compass spins, my directions laugh,
I ask a squirrel for a photograph.
He gives me looks, as if to say,
"Why not just lie in the sun all day?"

I chase the clouds, a kite in tow,
Where wisdom hides, I do not know.
But every pit stop brings a cheer,
And laughter drips like lemonade here.

So I'll roam free without a plan,
A song in my heart, just a simple man.
And if I find my dreams or meet,
I'll dance with joy on sticky feet.

The Allure of Empty Promises

They say the grass is greener there,
With fortune cookies filled with flair.
I bought a ticket to a show,
But ended up at a cow parade in snow.

Lured by tales of hidden gold,
I found a cat who looked quite old.
He winked and said, "Just take a nap,
Dream of riches in your lap!"

I chased bright lights, a fleeting thrill,
But ended up with an empty grill.
Yet every flop brings a new giggle,
As life serves up its lovely wiggle.

So I'll toast to dreams that fly away,
While munching on my buffet tray.
For laughter fills the heart with grace,
In the land of empty promises, a merry place.

Reflections in the Mist

I peeked into the world so sly,
Where reflections dance, and dreams go high.
But all I saw was my own face,
Making silly poses, just to embrace.

I chased shadows, thinking me wise,
But they all laughed with squinty eyes.
I bought a mirror named 'Revealer',
Turns out it was just a pizza dealer!

The mists rolled in with a comedic twist,
Where clarity's lost in a foggy mist.
I trip on ambitions that look so bright,
Yet roll away like a runaway kite.

So as I laugh at the foggy play,
I find my joy in the silly fray.
With reflections that tease, I learn to dance,
In the midst of confusion, I take a chance.

Questing in the Quicksand of Desire

Stuck in the muck of wants and needs,
I giggle at dreams like mischievous seeds.
I leapt for the stars, tripped on the moon,
Now here I sit with a vacuumed tune.

I reached for gold, grabbed a potato,
Which rolled away, dance like 'Nay-Nay-o'.
These treasures blur in a silly race,
As I wallow in quicksand, and find my space.

The more I pull, the deeper I go,
I might as well join the cactus show.
I spin and scoot, while others dig deep,
For in the muck, there's joy to keep.

So here's to those who lose their way,
Who find delight in the crazy play.
In quicksand patches, we find some fun,
With laughter bubbling like a soda run.

The Chase for Fleeting Whispers

I ran through the park where the squirrels play,
Chasing bright thoughts that danced away.
They hid in the bushes, giggling with glee,
Leaving me lost, just a puzzled old tree.

I tried asking pigeons what life had in store,
They cooed and they flapped, then flew out the door.
With breadcrumbs and dreams, I stopped for a bite,
But even my sandwich felt anxious tonight.

The flowers were laughing, what joke did I miss?
Twirling in colors that swirled like a bliss.
I thought I might ask the sun on the way,
But it just winked brightly and said, "Not today!"

So here I keep running, with giggles and sighs,
In search of the meaning while chasing the skies.
What if it's found in a cupcake delight?
Oh, where is my purpose? Just pass me a bite!

The Ballet of Unfounded Hope

I pirouetted off on a quest in my dreams,
Gliding on wishes, or so it seems.
The mirror reflected a dancer so grand,
But tripping on shoelaces was not what I'd planned.

I balanced on life's stage with a flair,
But my shoes were still squeaky, a dreadful affair.
The crowd looked confused, some laughed out aloud,
At a ballet of hopes in a mismatched crowd.

The set was all shaky, the lights flickered low,
As I leaped for my purpose, the encore, a show.
But instead of the claps, I heard just one squeal,
As a cat stole the spotlight, oh what a surreal!

Yet in all this chaos, I twirled with delight,
Who cares if I stumble, when laughter feels right?
My dreams may be chaotic, a topsy-turvy joke,
But in the grand ballet, it's fun to just poke!

Anchors in Shifting Tides

I set sail for fortune with a map in my hand,
But ended up stranded on the wrong shifting sand.
The captain's a seagull, with half an eye blinked,
And he squawked out directions; I pondered, then winked.

The waves sang a tune that was catchy, I swear,
But they led me in circles, an aquatic affair.
With anchors of marvel and tickles of cheer,
I wondered if purpose was just floating near.

The seaweed was dancing, quite merry and spry,
While the fish threw confetti and bubbles in high.
A jellyfish giggled, as it drifted along,
Maybe my quest was just this absurd song.

So here's to the anchors that bob in the tide,
Waving flags of nonsense, with nothing to hide.
Perhaps I'll just drift on this boat of the free,
And find that my purpose is simply to be!

Pursuing Light Through Gloom

I set off with a flashlight to chase down the dawn,
But the shadows kept tripping me, oh how they yawn.
The dark had its charms, like mischief and fun,
Yet I stumbled so often, I began to outrun.

The clouds wore silly hats, a carnival scene,
Each ray of the sun felt like a cheeky routine.
I laughed at my folly, both silly and grand,
As I danced with the gloom that had covered the land.

Old socks in the dryer still long for a pair,
Whispering secrets through the stale, musty air.
I followed their chatter, embraced all their quirks,
In the hunt for the light, found the joy in my smirks.

So onward I shimmied through murky old tales,
While the laughter of shadows swayed like the sails.
Next time I'll know better, all bright and aglow,
That light can be found just by letting it flow!

Waterfalls of Confusion

In a forest thick with trees,
I tripped over my shoelace,
Thought I found my destiny,
But it was just a rabbit's face.

Chasing dreams that make me giggle,
I mistook a taco for fate,
But it just got cold and wrinkled,
Now it's my funny dinner plate.

Huddled near the shining stream,
I pondered life's great mystery,
Dunked my toes in hopes and dreams,
Came out with just a blistered knee.

So I tumble down the hill,
With laughter echoing behind,
In this chaos, I get my fill,
Still fishing for that grand design.

The Hunt for a Vanishing Point

I set off on a daring quest,
A map that led to nowhere fast,
With all this jigging, what a jest,
Turns out it was a photo blast!

I climbed a high and twisted hill,
Thought I'd find a sign or clue,
But just a goat with quite the chill,
Gave me a laugh and then he flew!

I peeked inside a cornfield maze,
Searching for a glimmering view,
Step by step through these tall green ways,
Found a scarecrow, not much to do.

So I jazzed my soul with silly rhymes,
As I wandered without a care,
Putting all my hopes on dimes,
While chasing shadows everywhere.

Veils of Uncertainty

Behind curtains thick as fog,
I waved at some elusive goals,
Life feels like a lazy dog,
Rolling in a pile of shoals.

I donned a cape made of dreams,
Thinking I could fly so high,
But all I did was drop my creams,
And now my face looks like a pie.

I ponder on this cotton cloud,
Wishing for the stars to chat,
Yet finding whimsy, laughing loud,
As I realized I lost my hat.

So I tiptoe through life's soft fluff,
With giggles bubbling like a stream,
Each twist and turn just adds more stuff,
To this grand and dreamy scheme.

The Fabric of Lost Aspirations

In a attic packed with wishes,
I pulled out threads of ancient schemes,
Mixed them up with pasta dishes,
And stitched a quilt of silly dreams.

I wore a hat of great fortune,
But it just feigned to grant me luck,
Found spotty socks—a cute cartoon,
And tumbled like a clumsy duck.

In the middle of this fabric fun,
I wove a cape to wear with pride,
But with each spin, oh, what a run,
It turned into a bumpy ride.

So here I sit, a laugh and grin,
Surrounded by my quirky past,
In this tapestry, I spin,
Finding joy in threads that last.

The Ebb and Flow of Forgotten Passions

Once I tried to find my muse,
But my cat took all the views.
With a broomstick and a hat,
I danced with ghosts and fell flat.

Chasing dreams with mismatched socks,
While dodging squirrels on the blocks.
A pirate ship of laundry waits,
Where adventure and ironing debates.

I've learned my art in weird places,
Like when I painted with my braces.
Each splatter told a silly tale,
A masterpiece that starts to pale.

But here I laugh, and here I dwell,
In this circus, I bid farewell.
For every misstep, I've made a friend,
In the ebb and flow, the smiles won't end.

Breadcrumbs Leading Astray.

I scattered crumbs upon my path,
To catch a bit of fate or math.
But all I found were hungry birds,
And a few lost, confusing words.

I baked some pies with grand intent,
But only managed to ferment.
The recipe said 'just add glee,'
And now it smells like laundry, whee!

In search of wisdom, I was wise,
To shop in stores with blinking signs.
I bought a map that led to fun,
But all it showed was where to run.

Despite the chaos, here I stand,
With crumbs and laughter, not so bland.
For every wrong turn, I still embrace,
The thrill of life's absurd race.

Lost in Illusions

With a mirror and some sparkly glue,
I tried to find a better view.
But all I saw were silly looks,
Like cooking lessons from old books.

My dreams are sweet like cotton candy,
But float away, oh so dandy!
Reality's a slippery sheet,
I slip, I slide, just can't find my beat.

I wore a crown made out of tinfoil,
To rule the land of dreams that toil.
But every time I tried to reign,
I ended up playing silly games.

Yet in this fun perplexing dance,
I spin and twirl, I take the chance.
I'm lost in laughter, not in pain,
In this illusion, I'll remain.

Chasing Shadows at Dusk

I set out once to catch a dream,
With fishing rods and sunlit beams.
But shadows danced like wobbly jigs,
And tripped me up like funky gigs.

With a flashlight and my dancing shoes,
I thought I'd win at life's big cruise.
But shadows whispered silly things,
Like prancing rhinos with winged bling.

I ran in circles, round and round,
In pursuit of fun, where lost dreams found.
The night was young, the jokes were loud,
In every shadow, I felt so proud.

So here I chase with laughter bright,
Those playful shades in fading light.
In every misadventure, I see glee,
Chasing shadows, just being me.

Beneath the Surface of Longing

I tried my luck at the crystal ball,
But all it showed was a cat with a shawl.
Next, I picked up tarot cards in a spree,
Turns out they just spell 'sauce' for my tea.

In the back of a shop with a glowing sign,
I found a guru, he said I'd do fine.
But all his wisdom was about his last meal,
I left with a craving that was too real.

I wandered through forests with maps in my head,
Followed a squirrel who looked well-fed.
But each twist and turn led me to a tree,
I thought finding answers was better than free.

Now I sit with my coffee, a donut in hand,
Wondering where all my great plans had planned.
Finding joy in the snacks and the cafe vibe,
Maybe caffeine's the purpose I can describe.

The Labyrinth of the Heart

I took a path marked 'Happiness Found',
Ended up stranded on the ice cream mound.
Chased a balloon that was shaped like a heart,
But it popped and left me lost in the tart.

Instead of answers, I picked up some fries,
The secret to life, it seems, tastes like pies.
I turned to the stars, they twinkled with glee,
Yet all they advised was 'Just let it be.'

I thought to ask fate, but I tripped on the way,
Landed face-first in a party parade.
They handed me confetti and said, "What a treat!"
Turns out I'd discovered the gift of a beat.

So here I am laughing in circles of cheer,
Finding the silly, forgetting the fear.
In this riddle of lives, I'll wiggle and dance,
For joy isn't lost, it's just part of a chance.

Illusions of Destiny

I signed up for fortune, got a case of gloom,
Joined a circus, but all they found was room.
I twirled through the tent with a fake lion's roar,
Only to realize it was chasing for more.

With a magic eight ball, my guide in the night,
It said 'ask again', oh what a delight!
I tried all the angles, flipped it around,
All it could manage was a smirk and a frown.

I dove into books of epic sagas bold,
Misread the chapters, the secrets went cold.
So I penned my own fate with a pizza to bake,
Turns out destiny tastes great with some cake.

Laughter and toppings, my new guiding star,
I'm weaving through life with a slice, not a bar.
In the chaos, I found, with friends in the mix,
Destiny's finest is pizza and kicks.

Whispers in the Wind

The wind told me secrets, all wrapped in a breeze,
It promised adventure, with minimal fees.
I climbed up a mountain, thought I'd find gold,
Instead, just some squirrels, their chatter quite bold.

With each gust that played in my hair like a song,
I wondered if 'longing' had lasted too long.
I followed its whispers, my heart full of glee,
Only to trip over a root, yippee!

Where could I find answers to all of my quests?
The wind just sighed, suggesting more jest.
A bird flew ahead, with a great big laugh,
It pointed downwards, "Try a bubble bath!"

Now I soak in warm waters, with rubber ducks play,
Searching for wonders in a splashy ballet.
Purpose comes giggling with bubbles that rise,
In the joy of the moment, I find my surprise.

Among Shadows and Flickering Lights

In corners where the lost socks lay,
I ponder life in a quirky way.
A tangled thought from kitchen mess,
Try finding joy in this chaos, I guess.

The cat's my guide, with wisdom vast,
While fridge magnets cling to memories past.
A light bulb flickers, isn't it grand?
Is this the meaning I couldn't quite brand?

My coffee cup spills dreams on the floor,
Maybe I'm meant for something much more.
The world keeps spinning, laughter ensues,
Just another day of whimsical blues.

So here I stand, surrounded by quirk,
In a flashy hoodie with not much to work.
Perhaps my purpose is lost in plain sight,
Enjoying the shadows and flickering light.

Fleeting Dreams in the Twilight

A sandwich shared with ghosts of the night,
We chat about stars, oh what a delight!
But every bite tastes like yesterday's toast,
Do they serve purpose? I'm left to just boast.

In twilight's glow, I chase my own tail,
While ducks in the park start to unveil.
Do they know the secrets of life's gentle tease?
Or are they just wading, enjoying the breeze?

A fleeting thought does a pirouette,
What if my dreams are just one big regret?
Kites tangled high in the arboreal grasp,
I laugh as they tumble, no need to clasp.

So here's to the dusk and its whereabouts,
In shadows life whispers, amidst all the doubts.
With cookies and milk, today's menu is clear,
Let's groove with the chaos, we've nothing to fear!

Wandering, Always Wandering

I wandered off down the bread aisle,
Thought I'd find wisdom, at least a goodstyle.
But all I got was half-baked bread,
And questions that dance in my curly head.

With ants in my pants and shoes that squeak,
I find camaraderie with each lonely peak.
We laugh at the signs that point the wrong way,
Do they know we're lost? They just want to play.

A compass spins wildly, which way am I bound?
A squirrel scolds me, my focus unwound.
Perhaps this journey is errant delight,
A never-ending joke in the soft morning light.

So here I roam, with snacks in tow,
Discovering laughter in all that I don't know.
With maps made of candy and dreams on a string,
Maybe I'm wandering for the joy it can bring.

Echoes of the Unfulfilled

In the laundry room where hopes do spin,
I hear echoes of dreams, where do I begin?
Each sock speaks softly, of what could have been,
As I search for meaning in the lint-covered din.

The vacuum hums like a soothing refrain,
While I ponder my choices, and the mess in my brain.
Should I dance in pajamas, or put on a face?
In this kooky charade, I've found my true grace.

With echoes of laughter in the silence so deep,
I trip over thoughts that refuse to keep.
The mirror meanders, a crooked reflection,
Do bubbles and giggles hint at perfection?

So, I embrace the absurdity, the whims I have missed,
In every small moment, an ironic twist.
Perhaps being unfilled is the ultimate thrill,
As I roam through life's carnival, wild and ill.

Dreaming Among the Ruins

In the rubble, I found my keys,
They lead to a door that doesn't please.
Haunted by ghosts with outdated plans,
I barbecue with time's rusty cans.

The skyline's crooked, it smiles at me,
Where did I park my sense of glee?
A map that's scribbled, with crayons and fate,
I follow the path, but I'm always late.

My heart's a compass that points to fries,
In a world where adventure wears a disguise.
I trip on life's tongue, a comedy show,
The punchline arrives; I just don't know.

Among the ruins, I twirl and mock,
A jester in ruins, a wild-eyed clock.
I dance with the dust and laugh at the moon,
Who knew that despair would hum such a tune?

Shattered Reflections

A mirror cracked, my twin says hi,
But his style's outdated; I just roll my eyes.
We argue over who stole the cheese,
While reality dances, it's sure to tease.

Where do I go when the laughter fades?
To find my shadow in funny parades?
With every balloon that floats away,
I trip on the joy, come what may.

I tried to catch wisdom, it slipped like soap,
Tugging at fate's oversized rope.
I ponder the depths of jokes not told,
Each punchline a wish, each giggle gold.

In shattered reflections, I find what's lost,
Life serves me lemons from laughter's frost.
I toast to the flops, the messes I keep,
In the carnival of mishaps, I dive, not leap.

The Weight of Wandering

I bought a map, but it led me wrong,
To a dance with a toaster, now we sing its song.
I'm weighed down by moments of fleeting delight,
With breadcrumbs of laughter guiding my flight.

Chasing rainbows on a unicycle wheel,
Wandering earth in search of a meal.
I trip over options, too many to choose,
Each step is a riddle, each laugh is a bruise.

The weight of purpose is heavier still,
As I juggle my dreams, a lopsided thrill.
I build towers with coins from my stash,
But the bills keep laughing, don't let them clash.

In the circus of life, I juggle with pride,
While clowns in the corner just shake their heads wide.
Caught up in the motions, I laugh at the chase,
Life's one big joke, at quite the brisk pace.

Finding Echoes in Silence

In the quiet, I heard my shoe's last scream,
It echoed like whispers lost in a dream.
I searched through the stillness, my voice took flight,
It serenaded shadows 'til they turned bright.

The silence is loud, a comical mess,
It seems I'm the only one wearing finesse.
I tumble with mirrors that laugh in reply,
"Embrace the absurd, let it soar high!"

Footsteps of thoughts that dance around bends,
Each giggle's a letter from long-distance friends.
I collect all the chuckles that hang in the air,
Like balloons at a party, no worries or care.

Finding echoes, I dance with the breeze,
Twisting my fate with comical ease.
In the canopy of stillness, I twirl like a pro,
The punchline arrives, and I'm all aglow.

The Gaze of Hollow Stars

In a café filled with chatter, I sip my tea,
The universe laughs as I stumble, carefree.
A cat on a counter, judging my plight,
I ask for the moon, but settle for light.

I seek in the cosmos, a sign to behold,
While my socks are unmatched, a sight to unfold.
Constellations whisper of wisdom and fun,
But the best advice came from a dog on the run.

In gardens of laughter, the weeds dance around,
While I ponder deep thoughts where serenity's found.
A tree gives a nod, suggests I should stay,
And eat all the cookies, just don't ask for pay.

With stars in my eyes and confetti in hand,
I notice my shadow is building a band.
The hollow of night, a stage for my show,
Where I'm both the hero and comic, you know!

The Flight of Unseen Wings

A bird chirps loudly from inside my head,
Singing grand symphonies while I make my bed.
I sift through the pillows, my purpose in mind,
But just find a remote and some crumbs intertwined.

On a quest for meaning, I wear mismatched shoes,
Dancing in circles while I contemplate blues.
The floor is my canvas, my heart is the brush,
As I paint my own purpose in a colorful rush.

The fridge hums a tune, whispers secrets untold,
Suggesting adventures in pudding and mold.
I give it a nod, consider the game,
But my life's feeling more like a three-ringed shame.

I trip on the carpet, a flight to the floor,
To find meaning's a dance, but I just want more.
So I laugh with the chaos, I run with the whim,
For joy is the air beneath my unseen wing.

Chasing Flickers on the Wall

A shadow that winks as I turn on the light,
Flickers of purpose scurry out of sight.
Chasing reflections like they're on the run,
While the clock is just mocking, it's all in good fun.

I search for deep wisdom in half-eaten fries,
With dreams of success hidden deep in my pies.
The cat on the mantle starts plotting a scheme,
To convince me to chase all my wildest dreams.

In puddles of laughter, I splash through the day,
With my heart in my throat and my fears far away.
Each flicker a promise that shines bright and clear,
But they vanish like magic, replaced by cold beer.

Still, I giggle and wiggle, embracing the chase,
For life's little jokes are the heart of the race.
I'll follow those shadows 'til dawn breaks anew,
And declare that each laugh shows my purpose is true!

Paths Misdirected by Desire

On a road paved with dreams, I twirl and I spin,
But my GPS says I'm still lost within.
With crayons for mapping, I draw where I roam,
Each route leads to puddles, call them my home.

The map's full of scribbles, like a toddler's art,
While voicing my purpose feels like playing a part.
I dance with distractions, they're charmingly sly,
As ice cream sings sweetly to my wandering eye.

I lightheartedly trip on desires that gleam,
Candy-coated wishes that pop like a dream.
Each twist is a riddle; each turn is a plot,
Leading me spiraling, but laughs hit the spot.

So here I am stumbling, a jester's delight,
With a crown made of cupcakes and shoes full of light.
Misdirected by whims, I'll embrace every turn,
For joy's in the journey, let mischief discern!

Lost in the Labyrinth of Longing

In a maze of my own design,
I trip over dreams, oh so divine.
Climbing walls made of candy canes,
Where are my thoughts? All that remains?

A map made of jelly, it slips from my hand,
Turning left when I should take a stand.
Chasing my tail like a confused pup,
Oh look, there's a sign... wait, I've been here, yup!

Dancing with shadows that lead me astray,
While unicorns chuckle, 'Just another day!'
I poke at the clouds with a long, wooden stick,
Hoping they answer, but they just stay thick.

So I laugh at this wander, this whimsical quest,
For the joy of the stumble is what I love best.
In this comedy of errors, I'm destined to roam,
In a labyrinth of longing, I still feel at home.

The Mirage of Meaning

In the desert of doubt, I sip on air,
Finding great truths... or cactus despair.
With a mirage of wisdom dancing ahead,
I follow the sparkles, but I've lost my thread.

I leap over puddles of existential muck,
Hoping for clarity, but finding just luck.
A sage once said, 'It's all in your head,'
I nod, then I trip, and fall on my bed.

Running in circles, I find it quite neat,
To step in the rhythm of two left feet.
With each failed attempt, I chuckle and grin,
Oh where is the meaning, or did it just bin?

As I dust off the sand and check my old phone,
I realize the meaning is just being known.
And so in this mirage, I'll sip on that air,
Laughing and dancing with all kinds of flair.

Chasing Shadows of Ambition

I sprint after dreams like they're quicksilver,
But shadows are sly, they just make me shiver.
Ambition's a ghost that plays hide and seek,
With every mad chase, my approach feels weak.

I run into brick walls, just like a cartoon,
Bouncing right back, maybe I'll quit soon.
But the laughter of failure is such a delight,
Even if it's awkward, I'm still feeling bright.

With a hop and a skip, I chase down a crab,
Thinking it's fortune, but it's just a fab.
So I laugh at the wild, the odd, and bizarre,
Who knew ambition rides a spaceship-shaped car?

In this chase of the chilly, I find that I'm free,
For shadows are silly and don't bother me.
As I whirl through this chaos with a hearty big grin,
I discover the chase, and I'm happy within.

Echoes of Elusive Aspirations

Whispers of dreams bounce off outer walls,
Each echo a riddle; my mind takes a fall.
Aspirations giggle, like peas in a pod,
But catch me, oh dreams! You feel so odd.

Chasing reflections that sparkle and gleam,
They vanish like vapor, or so it would seem.
I shout to the ether, 'Hey, where's my goal?'
Only silence replies; I'm losing control.

Waltzing with hopes that slip through my hands,
They dance on the margin of enchanted lands.
With a twirl and a spin, I trip on my feet,
'One day you'll see me,' oh aspirations sweet.

Yet I giggle while pondering the strange,
For in this wild riddle, I'm happy to change.
The echoes may fade, but I'll always be bold,
In this laugh of confusion, my story unfolds.

The Ghosts of Ambition

In a land of empty dreams, I roam,
Chasing shadows that once felt like home.
With a map full of riddles and signs,
I trip on my own ambitious designs.

Balloons of bravado drift high in the air,
While my feet find solace in slumps of despair.
I saluted the stars, mistook scents for fate,
Now I'm stuck at the bus stop, feeling late.

I mistake my lunch for a grand banquet spread,
Steak made of hopes, but it's all in my head.
Giggles erupt when plans fall apart,
I'm the jester! What a whimsical art!

With a lantern of laughter, I light up the gloom,
In this circus of chaos, I craft my own room.
With jesters and dreams, I'm crafting my tale,
Falling up, not down, on this ridiculous scale.

Searching for Fire in the Rain

I wandered out with matches, prepared for a blaze,
But Mother Nature laughed and set me ablaze.
In puddles of purpose, I splashed and I flailed,
Looking for fire in the torrent that hailed.

The skies turned gray, like my attempts to ignite,
I tried coaxing warmth with a paper-thin light.
But the rain held secrets, like a moody chef,
Spicing my efforts, laughing like, 'Jeff, Jeff!'

Mirages of bonfires danced in my sight,
While I juggled a squelch in the dark of the night.
I caught a cold giggle from the clouds above,
They said, 'Why not dance? Forget all the love!'

So I spun in the downpour, twirling my dreams,
In the sizzle of lost hopes and whimsical beams.
Who needs a fire when you've got a good song?
I'll embrace the wet chaos and continue along.

The Paradox of Movement

I run in circles, feeling quite spry,
Chasing my tail while mimicking a fly.
With feet that are restless and thoughts that are whirr,
Each glorious march ends in an awkward slur.

I signed up for journeys through valleys and hills,
But ended up strolling through Life's dancing drills.
Steps that are grand, but where do they lead?
Just more clown shoes and a comedy seed.

In a desert of motion, I forgot how to walk,
Turned my daily grind into spur-of-the-chock.
Task lists like mazes with no cheese in a trap,
Leaving breadcrumbs of laughter on my mental map.

So here's to the race that never will start,
With my sneakers untied and my exuberant heart.
I'll twirl like a ballerina caught in a spin,
In this paradox of motion, I've learned to begin!

Unraveling the Jigsaw of Existence

Pieces splattered across the floor spread,
Trying to fit life's puzzle with a mismatched head.
I shoved in the corner where the cat had a nap,
Saying, 'This fits! Oh look, it's a cap!'

But the edges are missing, and the colors contrive,
Each moment I step back, I'm thankful I thrive.
With a grin and a giggle, I toss them around,
In this riddle of living, absurdity abounds.

I tried to define it, this whole crazy game,
Yet every "ah-ha" leads to more of the same.
In the jigsaw of chaos, I laugh at the race,
Stumbling on pieces, sprawled all over the place.

Perhaps it's not fitting, but a whimsical dance,
In the art of confusion, I'll take my chance.
With laughter my guide, I'll compose my own song,
In the jigsaw of existence, where all things belong.

Unraveled Threads of Meaning

In dreams, I found a treasure chest,
But all I got was a hula hoop.
I mistook my cat for a fortune-teller,
He just looked at me, then chased a loop.

I sought advice from the wise old tree,
It just whispered back, 'More coffee, please.'
The stars aligned for my cereal choice,
But it still led me to a bowl of peas.

I followed a squirrel on a whim today,
Hoping for answers, or maybe a snack.
But it jumped away, like it knew my plight,
Left me holding a small, empty sack.

I tried to read the clouds in the sky,
They all giggled back, "What's your next ploy?"
I danced with shadows, but they missed the beat,
Turns out my purpose was just to enjoy.

Where the Heart Strays

I thought love would bloom in the park's sweet grass,
But found a raccoon wearing my good sunglasses.
I asked for signs on a fortune cookie,
But all it said was, 'More soy, less Mookie.'

My heart wandered off to the local diner,
It left me behind with a pile of whiners.
I tried to find joy in chocolate and fries,
But the scales, my friend, had ulterior lies.

In the pursuit of bliss, I tried yoga too,
My downward dog turned into an 'upside do.'
The instructor laughed as I fell on my face,
Guess finding my zen was a slow-paced race.

I scoured the globe, but found only shoes,
Just my luck, no purpose, just bad news.
In this chaotic chase, I'll try not to pout,
For the heart may stray, but it's still worth the route.

The Recipe for Disillusion

I grabbed a book titled 'How to Succeed,'
But it was just a list of ways to mislead.
I mixed up some 'dreams' with 'a sprinkle of hope,'
But ended up draped in a spaghetti rope.

I tried to bake my ambitions all bright,
But they flopped like pancakes on a rainy night.
I whipped up a potion for zest and for zeal,
Got instead a concoction that resembled a meal.

My blender whirred with ideas galore,
But it spat out excuses, a hearty bore.
I dined with my fears, had dessert with doubt,
Turns out my menu was all mixed about.

With laughter I toss my foolish plans high,
For the recipe's only a whimsical lie.
I'll feast on the funny, let the chaos rise,
For life's tastiest bites are served with surprise.

Treading Water in Drowning Seas

I wore floaties to my big life quest,
Thought I'd surf the waves, oh what a jest!
Instead, I'm splashing in puddles so small,
With a rubber duck, my greatest pal.

I jumped in the deep end to find some flair,
But came up for air with hair filled with despair.
I tried to swim laps, like a dolphin on cue,
But I flopped like a fish out of love-scented glue.

I sought a lifeguard on the shore of my dreams,
But they just rolled their eyes, it seems.
I waved my arms wildly, making a scene,
But they responded, "You need a new routine."

In the current of life, I'll just ride the tide,
With laughter as my boat, I'll take it in stride.
For treading through laughter, though I feel the squeeze,
Might just turn the tide of my drowning seas.

Seeking Stars in Daylight

Caught a glimpse of glittering dreams,
But the sun was shining, or so it seems.
With shades on my nose and fries in hand,
I squint at the sky, not quite what I planned.

I wandered through alleys, lost in a trance,
Hoping to find the stars in a dance.
Instead, I found pigeons, what a delight!
They laughed at my quest, oh what a sight!

With ice cream melting and sandals that squeak,
I'm chasing the cosmos, or so I think.
But it's just a balloon that's floating away,
I chase it around, a bright yellow sway.

The laughter of kids rings clear in the park,
As I'm on the lookout for some shining spark.
Yet the stars I sought were out of my view,
Guess I'll settle for clouds, and ice cream too!

Mirrors Reflecting False Truths

Stood in front of mirrors, quite a few,
Hoping to find something shiny and new.
Instead, my hair's a wild, frizzy crown,
Reflecting my hopes while I'm upside down.

Tried to dig deeper, found only a mess,
That freshly painted smile, I must confess.
The real me's hiding behind all the glass,
Yet my reflection keeps playing the sass.

Caught in a tangle, oh what a scene,
Twisting and turning like I'm on a screen.
"Look at this beauty!" I cried with glee,
But the mirror just winked back at me.

So I'll strut my stuff like a peacock, bold,
If the glass can't hold true, then I'll just be sold.
Wandering through worlds made of shiny lies,
I'll laugh with my mirrors, much to my surprise!

Chasing the Wind's Embrace

I ran with the breeze, oh what a thrill,
Thought I'd catch whispers, a whispering chill.
But it laughed at my sneakers, so light, so fast,
As I tumbled and turned, tried to run, but alas!

With a kite in my hands, I soared up so high,
While the wind played tag, I was ready to fly.
Yet every time I threw out my string,
The kite tangled my thoughts, what a goofy fling.

Twirled and swirled in a playful ballet,
The gusts teased me gently, then whisked me away.
"I'll catch you, dear Wind!" I shouted with glee,
But it just blew a kiss and left me to flee.

So I danced in the sunlight, chasing my tail,
Following echoes of laughter and wail.
While I grasped at the air, so wild and free,
The wind rolled its eyes, laughing at me!

Forks in Roads Untraveled

At the fork in the road, what a peculiar sight,
Two paths diverged, both wrapped in twilight.
One led to tacos, the other to pie,
I stood there confused, just wanting to try.

With a map that was printed on bubble-wrap dreams,
I weighed my decisions in whimsical schemes.
But both paths called out, "Choose us, oh please!"
I danced between them like I was on keys.

Should I chase after tacos or go for a slice?
Each fork a dilemma, oh wouldn't that be nice?
But my stomach just rumbled, it wanted some treats,
I giggled and skipped, letting whimsy lead me.

So I took the road marked with sparkle and heaps,
Found joy on the journey where laughter creeps.
At the end of the path was a feast so divine,
"Why not both?" I grinned, "Now that's how I shine!"

Whispers of the Uncharted

In a thrift store I wandered, how odd,
Hoping to find my life's little prods.
A cat sweater's allure, it held me in place,
As I tripped over dreams wrapped up in lace.

The fortune teller laughed, with a sparkle in eye,
Said my future was bright, 'til I asked her why.
She pointed to tacos, a taco stand near,
So I took a detour, let out a loud cheer.

Maps drawn in crayon, all colors gone wild,
I chased after rainbows, like a hungry child.
With pinwheels of wishes, I danced with delight,
And found my true calling was just out of sight.

Now I sit with a sandwich, perplexed but content,
While the universe giggles, on my path I'm bent.
With pickle jar wisdom, I write out my tale,
Life's purpose in laughs, it'll never grow stale.

Flickering Flames of Discontent

With candles a-blazing, I sought after bliss,
Instead, I found cats that had grown quite amiss.
Their mischief, a dance at the top of the stairs,
Left me contemplating the meaning of bears.

I dived into YouTube for wisdom and fun,
Learned how to juggle while burning the bun.
A life coach advised I should stand on my head,
While I pondered if toast was my true heart's spread.

Amongst the confusion, a light bulb went off,
I'd cook up a casserole and never feel soft.
With kitchen disasters, I gathered great cheer,
And served up my heart on a plate, oh so dear.

So here's to the moments that make us feel lost,
With laughter and crumbs, we can pay any cost.
In the flickers of flames, I'll ask, "What's the deal?"
While I roll my eyes at what's part of the meal.

A Dance in the Desert of Dreams

In the desert of wishes, I bust out a jig,
Swirling like cacti, and feeling quite big.
I dreamt of a kettle, that sang me a tune,
But it turned out to whistle with none of the boom.

My compass was spinning, a real sight to see,
When I took a wrong turn at a cactus tree.
A mirage appeared, with a lemonade stand,
But all that I got was a cup full of sand.

I tango'd with tumbleweeds, swaying with grace,
Wishing for guidance in this vast, empty space.
A snappy old lizard gave me quite the grin,
"Just dance through the nonsense, let the fun begin!"

So I twirled my way home, under stars all aglow,
With mismatched old flip-flops, I found my own flow.
In the dance of the sand, I discovered my pride,
Sometimes the wrong step's the best place to glide.

The Siren Song of Misguided Paths

Bewitched by a radio, its tunes full of sass,
I followed the rhythm, and found quite a class.
To learn the fine art of banana ballet,
Signing up for mischief, I flailed all the way.

I took a few wrong turns in my bright yellow boots,
Encountering rhinos, and singing the blues.
With every misstep, I chuckled and snorted,
As my purpose eluded, but giggles still sorted.

A guide made of jellybeans led me astray,
At the end of each rainbow, I bid friends a "hey."
With gummy bears cherishing my confused plight,
I dove into cupcakes, oh what a sweet night!

While searching for meaning, I found balloon art,
In the mishmash of chaos, I dug up my heart.
So cheers to the songs that lead us amiss,
For the laughter we find is the ultimate bliss.

www.ingramcontent.com/pod-product-compliance
Lightning Source LLC
Chambersburg PA
CBHW071836160426
43209CB00003B/316